The Anatomy of UNITY and

DIVISION

Mark B. Pape

2025: One Stone Press.
All rights reserved. No part of this book may be reproduced
in any form without written permission of the publisher.

Published by:
One Stone Press
979 Lovers Lane
Bowling Green, KY 42103

Printed in the United States of America

ISBN: 978-1-966992-13-4

1(800)428-0121
www.onestone.com

Contents

Forward		5
1	The Unity of The Father, Son & Holy Spirit	7
2	The Divine Perspective of Unity for Man	13
3	Jesus' Death—The Cost of Religious Unity	17
4	The Bible—The Only Basis for Religious Unity	23
5	Motives That Cause Religious Division	29
6	Methods Used to Divide	33
7	The Collateral Damage of Religious Division	39
8	The Only Justifiable Cause for Religious Division	45
9	The Scriptural Solution for Division	51
10	Preservation of Congregational Unity	59
11	Eternal Consequences of Division	67
12	The Reward of Unity	71
13	Review	75

Forward

Division in the church of Christ is an ugly sin. It disgraces the Great God and His Son, whom we serve, and the Holy Spirit who searched the mind of God and delivered the message of unity. I have seen those whom I respected change colors like a chameleon, and unveil speech and conduct only becoming of the devil. And, this was for the purpose of promoting division. Division angers the Heavenly Father, and it should anger anyone who claims to be His faithful child. Proverbs 6:19 should cause the Christian much consternation if they have been involved in promoting division in the church. Why? Rounding off the list of seven things God hates is *"And one who sows discord among brethren."*

Developing these lessons has forced me to consider people, places, and events during my spiritual journey that I would rather not remember. From my experience and those shared by others, it is my conviction that congregations must proactively study the preservation of unity and the causes of division to prevent it. Elders must be aggressive in protecting congregations from the slightest matter that may develop into something divisive. I have never seen a "problem" in the church become better when ignored. It always festers into a sore that retroactive action rarely heals, but proactive measures may have prevented it.

The Anatomy of Unity and Division is offered with prayer and hope that in some small way it may help congregations quench the fiery darts of the wicked one. And, should this occur, *"to Him be glory in the church by Christ Jesus to all generations, forever and ever. Amen"* (Eph. 3:21).

Mark B Pape
October 2025

In appreciation:
Many thanks to Peggy Dodds of Newbern Tennessee for her extensive efforts with grammatical quality and proof-reading.

Introduction

Nothing unnerves me more than learning of a rupture in a congregation of the Lord's Church over non-scriptural matters. I have endured it first hand and heard others with these sad reports, all of which bear the same evil trademarks. My objective with the design of this workbook is fourfold: 1. To extol the unity of the Father, the Son, and the Holy Spirit as our pattern for unity. 2. Explore the plain commands of God for His people to be unified. 3. Identify the means and motives of division. 4. To understand that division can, and must be healed.

Congregations and elders who ignore the possibility that Satan is always actively plotting division are sadly mistaken. This attitude will eventually result in division and all its consequences, which are much more challenging to repair than to prevent. Fiercely preserving unity, identifying the early warning signs of division and dealing with them is my hope and prayer for all congregations of the Church of Christ. If this study helps in some small way, may God and His Son receive all glory and praise.

Mark B Pape

The Anatomy of Unity and Division

Lesson One

The Unity of the Father—the Son—and the Holy Spirit

Besides the Father, the Son, and the Holy Spirit, there has never been, nor will there ever be any assembly of beings more unified than they. Their seamless unity cannot be duplicated among men, because they are perfect, unblemished, and without the characteristics mortals develop through the process of temptation and subsequently sinning. The diagram below illustrates the three individual Persons of the Godhead, and the synchronization of their intertwined roles.

To use human terms, the Father is the Superintendent of the Divine enterprise, especially regarding the redemption of man. *"There is...one God and Father of all, who is above all, and through all, and in you all"* (Eph. 4:6).

The Godhead's unity is demonstrated by the Father's delegation of all authority to His Son Jesus, and Jesus' willingness to accept and discharge this responsibility as His Father wills. *"All authority has been given to Me in heaven and on earth"* (Matt. 28:18). Jesus will retain this authority until the end of time. *"Then comes the end, when He delivers the kingdom to God the Father, when He puts an end to all rule and all authority and power. For He must reign till He has put all enemies under His feet"* (1 Cor. 15:24-25). The Father and Son's seamless unity is clearly visible because Jesus submitted to His Father's will.

Jesus accepted the role delegated to Him in view of the investment He would make one day. The Father sent His Son to earth to pay the cost to redeem man from eternal ruin because he had sinned. *"Knowing that you were not redeemed with corruptible things, like silver or gold, from your aimless conduct received by tradition from your fathers, but with the precious blood of Christ, as of a lamb without blemish and without spot" (1 Pet. 1:18-19).*

The Holy Spirit's role was to reveal what the Father wants man to know that had not been previously made known. This revelation includes the Father's scheme to redeem man and the conditions man must meet. *"But God has revealed them to us through His Spirit. For the Spirit searches all things, yes, the deep things of God. For what man knows the things of a man except the spirit of the man which is in him? Even so no one knows the things of God except the Spirit of God" (1 Cor. 2:10-11).*

> **Jesus and His Father are one because of Jesus' selfless and unwavering submission to His Father's will. Without such surrender, division between them would have been inevitable.**

Paul further elaborates how the Holy Spirit would share the mystery of the ages, and that it can be known when read, *"How that by revelation He made known to me the mystery (as I have briefly written already, by which, when you read, you may understand my knowledge in the mystery of Christ), which in other ages was not made known to the sons of men, as it has now been revealed by the Spirit to His holy apostles and prophets: that the Gentiles should be fellow heirs, of the same body, and partakers of His promise in Christ through the gospel," (Eph. 3:3-6).*

In the above diagram, the three circles represent the three individuals of the Godhead. The intersection of these circles represents the overlapping, unified, and interlocked work they exert for our redemption and salvation. There is no division among them in their mission, roles, or work. Jesus speaks to the unity He and the Father have when He prayed to the Father, *"Now I am no longer in the world, but these are in the world, and I come to You. Holy Father, keep through Your name those* whom You have given Me, that they may be one as We are" (John 17:11). Jesus made the same statement to His disciples in John 10:30, *"I and My Father are one."*

Jesus and His Father are one because of Jesus' selfless and unwavering submission to His Father's will. Without such surrender, division between them would have been inevitable. Jesus unashamedly confesses His giving over of His will three times in John 5 when He says, *"I can of Myself do nothing. As I hear, I judge; and My judgment is righteous, because I do not seek My own will but the will of the Father who sent Me" (John 5:30).*

The unity of the Father and Son is seen from the Creation until Jesus' earthly arrival. John wrote, *"In the beginning was the Word, and the Word was with God, and the Word was God. He was in the beginning with God. All things were made through Him, and without Him nothing was made that was made" (John 1:1-3).* Verse 14 defines exactly who the Word is: *"And the Word became flesh and dwelt among us, and we beheld His glory, the glory as of the only begotten of the Father, full of grace and truth."*

Moving forward to the age of the prophets, we see their knowledge was limited, though they searched for answers to their questions about God's ultimate plan to save man. *"Of this salvation the prophets have inquired and searched carefully, who prophesied of the grace that would come to you, searching what, or what manner of time, the Spirit of Christ who was in them was indicating when He testified beforehand the sufferings of Christ and the glories that would follow" (1 Pet. 1:10-11).* Peter writes that Jesus, though not revealing all the details, was empowering them to offer hope through the arrival of a suffering Savior. Peter would also write, *"knowing this first, that no prophecy of Scripture is of any private interpretation, for prophecy never came by the will of man, but holy men of God spoke as they were moved by the Holy Spirit" (1 Pet. 1:20-21).*

Man could never have known or imagined the unity of the Father, Son, and Holy Spirit had not the Holy Spirit been commissioned to reveal what we can know from the New Testament including Jesus is the creative Word, the Father sent Jesus to earth to reveal to us what deity looks like from the human perspective, and that the Gospel is the exclusive message revealed to redeem man. In John 14, Jesus elaborates on His relationship with the Father using statements like, *"If you had known Me, you would have known My Father also; and from now on you know Him and have seen Him...He who has seen Me has seen the Father,"* and

"Believe Me that I am in the Father and the Father in Me, or else believe Me for the sake of the works themselves" (John 14:7, 9, 11).

Jesus and the Father are not the same being, but one in purpose, mission, planning, and their ultimate goal to save man. The nature of the Father, the Son and the Holy Spirit's s unified relationship is related to us by the Holy Spirit in the first sentence of the book of Hebrews, *"God, who at various times and in various ways spoke in time past to the fathers by the prophets, has in these last days spoken to us by His Son, whom He has appointed heir of all things, through whom also He made the worlds; who being the brightness of His glory and the express image of His person, and upholding all things by the word of His power, when He had by Himself purged our sins, sat down at the right hand of the Majesty on high" (Heb. 1:1-3).*

Conclusion

We have briefly examined a sampling of what the Bible reveals regarding the unity of the Father, the Son, and the Holy Spirit. Their unity resulted in the planning and creation of the world and man, the preservation of the human family until Christ would come, the redemption of man, and the ushering in of the Gospel to save man. As we will see in further studies, this divine example of unity is a pattern for God's people today. In its absence, the cause of Christ is hindered, and the souls of some saints and all sinners are doomed.

Questions and Discussion

1. What prevents men from having the same unity as the Father, the Son, and the Holy Spirit?

2. Define the roles of the Father, the Son, and the Holy Spirit.

3. How is the unity of the Father and Son demonstrated? And, what characteristics of Jesus make this unity possible?

4. For what specific cause does the Bible reveal that the Father, the Son, and the Holy Spirit are unified?

5. Explain the roles of, and how the Father, the Son and the Holy Spirit were unified in the creation of the world.

6. From 1 Peter 1:11-12, how were the prophets informed with the limited information they received? Who else desired to know more?

7. From John 17:11, how does Jesus pray that we will imitate Him and the Father? How is this achieved?

8. From Hebrews 1:1-3, discuss how Jesus and His Father are compared.

9. From John 14-16, study each mention of the Holy Spirit. Discuss His role, who will dispatch Him, and for what reasons.

10. From 1 Cor. 2:10-15, discuss the work of the Holy Spirit, how He obtains the information He imparts to man, and the nature of this information.

11. List those things the Father, the Son, and the Holy Spirit have been unified in that you enjoy the results of today.

Lesson Two

The Divine Perspective of Unity for God's People

There can be no doubt that King David shared the sentiments of the Heavenly Father when he wrote, *"Behold, how good and how pleasant it is for brethren to dwell together in unity" (Psa. 133:1).* God wants and demands His people dwell together in unity. And He provides everything necessary to make this possible. No greater investment has ever been made than God's gift of His Son so men can be unified with Him and with one another. As studied in Lesson 1, the Godhead demonstrates the perfect pattern of unity for men to imitate.

To believe, or teach, unity among God's people is impossible is to disagree with God, Christ, the Holy Spirit and Their inspired words. Why? Because the inspired Apostle Paul wrote that God provided all things necessary. *"And He Himself gave some to be apostles, some prophets, some evangelists, and some pastors and teachers, for the equipping of the saints for the work of ministry, for the edifying of the body of Christ, till we all come to the unity of the faith and of the knowledge of the Son of God, to a perfect man, to the measure of the stature of the fullness of Christ" (Eph. 4:11-13).* The days of the Apostles and Prophets are long gone. Therefore, the unity of the faith and knowledge of the Son of God rests on the shoulders of evangelists, pastors, and teachers when they teach and make application of the word of God. The unity God commands is on no other basis. Only God can provide what is needed to meet His definition of unity. God's perspective of unity is not optional, regardless of how difficult it may be. His instrument to unite all people in every nation is the Gospel. When the Gospel is taught, believed, and obeyed, it will produce nothing except unity. The Gospel is a singular message from a Godhead that is unified. It is not the product of human thinking, wants, or desires. When the Gospel is deviated from, division is inevitable. We shall consider this truth in greater detail in Lesson 4.

Would Jesus pray for something He knew was impossible? Of course not. This is why He prayed, *"Holy Father, keep through Your name those whom You have given Me, that they may be one as We are" (John 17:11).* Paul echoes the sentiments of his Lord when he writes, *"Now may the God of patience and comfort grant you to be like-minded toward one another, according to Christ Jesus, that you may with one mind and one mouth glorify the God and Father of our Lord Jesus Christ" (Rom.*

15:5-6). The oneness Jesus prayed for, and the Father demands is not "agreeing to disagree," but all having the single mindedness that they have. Any other definition or method does not meet divine expectation. The church at Philippi was a praiseworthy congregation. Yet, Paul does not hesitate to remind them by inspiration that unity must continue to be guarded and preserved, and he tells them how this is achieved. *"Only let your conduct be worthy of the gospel of Christ, so that whether I come and see you or am absent, I may hear of your affairs, that you stand fast in one spirit, with one mind striving together for the faith of the gospel"* (Phil. 1:27).

A real question at the core of our topic is: What is God's perspective of those who cause division? He has zero tolerance for anyone who leads, aids, and abets the unscriptural dividing of His people. And, the Bible contains no more severe warnings than those against the perpetrators of division. When the Proverb writer reveals the *"six things the Lord hates, yes, seven are an abomination to Him"* the bookend concluding the list is, *"and one who sows discord among brethren"* (Prov. 6:16-19). The word *"hate"* in this text carries with it the idea of an enemy. Being an enemy of God is a losing proposition.

> *Would Jesus pray for something He knew was impossible? Of course not. This is why He prayed, "Holy Father, keep through Your name those whom You have given Me, that they may be one as We are" (John 17:11).*

As you would expect, Jesus was not silent on this matter either. He shares the same perspective about unity and division among God's people as His Father. Although Jesus prayed for unity among His believers, He also spoke to the inevitability that divisions would come. He shared His view of those causing division with His disciples. *"It is impossible that no offenses should come, but woe to him through whom they do come! It would be better for him if a millstone were hung around his neck, and he were thrown into the sea, than that he should offend one of these little ones"* (Luke 17:1-2). The word *"woe"* used by Jesus is a term of denunciation, and easy to understand in the context of the spiritual death sentence of being thrown into the sea, with a millstone tied about the neck. Jesus' authority would be appealed to by Paul in the first few sentences of his letter to the Corinthians. This divided church was veering away from the pattern God has for unity among His people. They were not functioning within the authority of Jesus Christ. Paul commanded to take remedial action and how to take it. *"Now I plead with you, brethren, by the name of our Lord Jesus Christ, that you all speak the same thing, and that there be no divisions among you, but that you be perfectly joined together in the same mind and in the same judgment" (1 Cor. 1:10).* He asks them, *"is Christ divided."* This question should bring the matter of division among God's people into clear focus.

Conclusion

The Bible is replete with commands and examples of God's perspective on unity among His people. They are easy to understand and not optional. Jesus is the King, and we are His subjects. He is the one Lawgiver; we have no legislative role in His Kingdom. He bought the church; the church is His people. They must believe and act in accordance with His will, or suffer the eternal consequence.

Questions For Discussion

1. What is the divine example of how God's people are to be unified?

2. In what two ways are we to be unified?

3. Why is it sinful to believe or teach that God's people cannot be unified?

4. What has God provided so that we can be unified?

5. Discuss the verses in Jesus' prayer in John 17 that address His will for the unity of believers.

6. What is the Heavenly Father's disposition regarding those causing division? Review and discuss the texts supporting your answer.

7. What is Jesus' disposition regarding those causing division? Review and discuss the texts supporting your answer.

8. What was Paul's inspired remedy for the division in the church at Corinth? See 1 Cor. 1:10

9. Discuss the nature of a king, the kingdom's law and the king's expectation for his citizens as it relates to the Kingdom of Christ.

Lesson Three

Jesus' Death—The Cost of Religious Unity

Nothing more clearly convey the value of something more than the cost someone is willing to pay for it. The death of God's only Son to redeem man not only declares the value of the soul but also the cost God was willing to pay for man to have unity with Him. We think of death as a separation. However, without the death of Christ, unity with the Father would be impossible.

As we study the cost of religious unity, we must define the word "religion." It is only used five times in the Bible, all of which are found in the New Testament. (N.T.) The word "religion" as used by the author of this lesson means, "the system of faith revealed in the N. T. for people who desire to please God, have unity with Him and with fellow believers."

Jesus was sent to this world to die, and afterwards was authorized by the Father to author a system of faith (religion) to reconcile man with God. Paul wrote that the Gospel (good news) he preached to the Corinthians began with Jesus dying. *"For I delivered to you first of all that which I also received: that Christ died for our sins according to the Scriptures, and that He was buried, and that He rose again the third day according to the Scriptures" (1 Cor. 15:3-4).* As we consider Jesus' death in these verses, it is not meant to depreciate His burial and resurrection, which Paul also mentioned. However, a sacrifice was required that would placate God's wrath against sin and those who commit it. His sacrifice enabled man to be unified with God. The salvation of man was God's objective from the time man sinned in the Garden of Eden until Jesus came to earth to die for it. *"Though He was a Son, yet He learned obedience by the things which He suffered. And having been perfected, He became the author of eternal salvation to all who obey Him" (Heb. 5:8-9).*

Before the sacrifice of Jesus, animal sacrifices were authorized by God, but they did not have the power to alleviate man's long-term problem of sin entirely. *"For it is not possible that the blood of bulls and goats could take away sins" (Heb. 10:4).* If those sacrifices could not take away sin, how would the problem be resolved? Earlier in this same writing the author makes the contrast that brings into clearer focus why a better sacrifice was needed to unify man with God, *"For if the blood of bulls and goats and the ashes of a heifer, sprinkling the unclean, sanctifies for* the purifying of the flesh, how much more shall the blood of Christ, who through the eternal Spirit offered Himself without spot to God, cleanse your conscience from dead works to serve the living God" (Heb. 9:13-14).

A New Testament word describing one aspect of our unity with God is "reconcile," which means, "to change from an enemy to friend" (Vines). Reconciliation was not cheap. It came at a high cost we are incapable of paying. *"And by Him to reconcile all things to Himself, by Him, whether things on earth or things in heaven, having made peace through the blood of His cross. And you, who once were alienated and enemies in your mind by wicked works, yet now He has reconciled in the body of His flesh through death, to present you holy, and blameless, and above reproach in His sight"* (Col. 1:20-22). To be changed from an enemy to a friend of God, one must be reconciled to Him on His terms. As is the case in the above verses, when reconciliation is mentioned in the N. T., the death of

Unity with God and one another is not optional if we expect to be saved. Any division between man and God results in everlasting separation from Him. Any division among His people will cost someone their soul, because they did not appreciate the cost paid to make unity possible.

Jesus is almost always either stated or implied. The clause, *"the blood of His cross,"* is used to define the cost and purpose of Jesus' death. The price was the cross (death), the purpose was to make peace with God, i.e., unity. Jesus' death makes it possible to be a friend of God. Again, Paul writes, *"and that He might reconcile them both to God in one body through the cross, thereby putting to death the enmity"* (Eph. 2:16). Jews and Gentiles alike must be added to the one body provided by Jesus' death. Unity with God is not possible in more than one body because there is only one body that He recognizes (Eph. 4:4). The one body we are reconciled into is the church (Eph. 1:22). Jesus' death even redeemed and reconciled the obedient who lived under the previous covenant. *"And for this reason, He is the Mediator of the new covenant, by means of death, for the redemption of the transgressions under the first covenant, that those who are called may receive the promise of the eternal inheritance"* (Heb. 9:15).

Conclusion

As we consider the extreme cost the Father and Son paid so that we may be unified with them, we should therefore forge in our minds the importance of being unified with one another. Unity with God and one another is not optional if we expect to be saved. Any division between man and God results in everlasting separation from Him. Any division among His people will cost someone their soul, because they did not appreciate the cost paid to make unity possible. *"Anyone who has rejected Moses' law dies without mercy on the testimony of two or three witnesses. Of how much worse punishment, do you suppose, will he be thought worthy who has trampled the Son of God underfoot, counted the blood of the covenant by which he was sanctified a common thing, and insulted the Spirit of grace"* (Heb. 10:28-29).

Questions and Discussion

1. How can we understand the value God places on our unity with Him and our unity with one another?

2. What does the word "religion" mean as it relates to this study, and how does this word help us understand our relationship with God?

3. What qualified Jesus to author a system of religion?

4. How many religions or systems of faith did Jesus author that will unify man with God (Heb. 5:9, 12:2; Eph. 4:3-6)?

The Anatomy of Unity and Division

5. How do men become unified with the Father and Son in the one body or religion (Acts 2:47)?

6. What made peace between God and man possible (Col. 1:22-23)?

7. Explain how the death of Jesus should unify members of Christ's church?

8. When the word "blood" occurs in the N. T. regarding Jesus, what is it usually considering? Give examples.

9. List at least four things this lesson considers that we obtain by Christ's death.

10. How does the word "reconciliation" describe the nature of unity between God and man?

11. What cost was paid, and who paid it, so we can be reconciled with God (Col. 1:20-23; Eph. 2:16; Rom. 5:10)?

Jesus' Death—The Cost of Religious Unity

12. Into what is man reconciled (Col. 1:20-22; Eph. 2:16)?

13. When the words "reconcile, reconciled, or reconciliation" appear in scripture, what theme is usually under consideration in the same context?

14. From Heb. 9:15, how have those who lived under the first covenant benefited from the death of Christ?

15. As you consider the cost of your redemption, what impact should this have on your efforts to preserve unity with your brethren?

16. From Heb. 10:28-29, what must one conclude about God's attitude regarding the cost He and Christ paid for unity?

17. Discuss how the Lord's Supper (memorializing Jesus' body, blood and death) should prompt one to think about reconciliation with God.

18. Where does the person with questions about being unified with God find true answers? Where can he be sure the answers are false?

Lesson 4

The Bible—The Only Basis for Religious Unity

The idea of God sending Christ to die to save man, inaugurate His religion, and not provide a basis for its unity is unthinkable, and completely out of character for the Godhead. Every discipline we pursue in the physical realm appeals to a standard. These include engineering, medicine, science, and other fields. From time to time, because man is fallible, he learns the basis for his actions are established on an incorrect standard. He then modifies his practice to match what is true, so he can achieve the desired result. Just the opposite is the case in the spiritual realm. Its Author is perfect and only needed to design the spiritual standard one time. No revision was required to achieve His desired results. In fact, many times the Bible pronounces curses on those who tamper with His revealed spiritual truths—the Bible.

There can never be religious unity in the human family unless all appeal to God's one revealed truth. Jesus prayed for the unity of His disciples in John 17, and then for those (including us) who believe in Him through their word. *"I do not pray for these alone, but also for those who will believe in Me through their word; that they all may be one, as You, Father, are in Me, and I in You; that they also may be one in Us, that the world may believe that You sent Me" (John 17:20-21)*. So, Jesus prayed that we might be one *"through their words."* Is this possible? If not, why would Jesus have prayed for such? These *"words"* needed to unify believers were never the product of a man. They were from the mind of God as revealed by the Holy Spirit. These *"words"* were conveyed to men to preach and write, and are preserved for us in what we call the Bible. Religious division is so rampant because men either disbelieve or ignore the revealed message, or believe they have the right to design and implement their own standard.

Immediately preceding Jesus' prayer recorded in John 17, He promised His apostles three times that they would be guided into all truth by the Holy Spirit. (see John 14:25-26, 15:26, and 16:5-15) Did Jesus follow through with His promise? If so, then why do men preach, teach, believe, and obey doctrines that are completely foreign to the revealed message contained in the Bible? These foreign doctrines originate with men, not God. Jesus quoted Isaiah when He said, *"These people draw near to Me with their mouth, and honor Me with their lips, but their heart is far from*

Me. And in vain they worship Me, teaching as doctrines the commandments of men" (Matt. 15:8-9). Teaching the commandments and doctrines of men is sinful because the false teacher is usurping a role for which only God is qualified. A false teacher puts himself in opposition to God. God has never authorized a man to create or author a system of faith or a religion. Neither has He ever consulted a man when drafting a covenant or law for man to live by. Only that which was revealed through the Holy Spirit is capable of unifying man with God.

Paul understood the exclusive right of Jesus as the author of the one gospel, and rebuked the Galatians for veering away from it. He wrote, *"I marvel that you are turning away so soon from Him who called you in the grace of Christ, to a different gospel, which is not another; but there are some who trouble you and want to pervert the gospel of Christ. But even if we, or an angel from heaven, preach any other gospel to you than what*

> **When an honest person learns their faith, worship, religion, or doctrine is inconsistent with the Bible, they will repent and conform to the truth. The dishonest person does not change his course, but seeks to justify himself.**

we have preached to you, let him be accursed" (Gal. 1:6-8). Paul did not exempt himself from being accursed if found preaching another gospel than the one revealed to him by the Lord. In this same context, he wrote, *"But I make known to you, brethren, that the gospel which was preached by me is not according to man. For I neither received it from man, nor was I taught it, but it came through the revelation of Jesus Christ" (Gal. 1:11-12).* Paul emphasizes that the source of what he had taught them was from the Lord, not himself, an angel or any other man. Why? Because the only gospel that unifies man with God is the one gospel revealed from heaven. When Jesus was asked by the chief priests, scribes, and elders, *"By what authority are you doing these things?"* Jesus replied, *"The baptism of John—was it from heaven or from men?" (Mark 11:27-30).* This is the test for any religious doctrine today. Is it from heaven or men? This determines whether a doctrine should be heeded or dismissed. It is the doctrines of men or man's perversion of God's word that cause religious division.

To be sure, we are investing our faith in what God has revealed that He wants. Only He can provide what unifies us with Him. We must seek only His scriptures and never entertain anything from any other source. In his instructions to Timothy, Paul writes, *"All Scripture is given by inspiration of God, and is profitable for doctrine, for reproof, for correction, for instruction in righteousness, that the man of God may be complete, thoroughly equipped for every good work" (2 Tim. 3:16-17)*. The word *"inspiration"* literally means *"God breathed."* God breathed information (scripture) can be found in no other source than the Bible. Given the adequacy of *"all scripture given by God,"* men waste their time and anger God with their attempts to change or improve it.

How can a person prove their religious practices are unified with God's will? The answer is *"Test all things; hold fast what is good. Abstain from every form of evil" (1 Thes. 5:21-22)*. Put the question to the test of the Bible. In other words, "prove it." Is it good and acceptable because God says so, or because men say so? Paul instructed the Roman Christians, *"And do not be conformed to this world, but be transformed by the renewing of your mind, that you may prove what is that good and acceptable and perfect will of God" (Rom. 12:2)*. Many today refuse to accept the fact that there are false teachers. This denial is dangerous. These same people think if someone believes in Jesus, everything else is just minutia. Peter did not think so when he wrote, *"But there were also false prophets among the people, even as there will be false teachers among you, who will secretly bring in destructive heresies, even denying the Lord who bought them, and bring on themselves swift destruction" (2 Peter 2:1)*. When a person hears a doctrine that sounds new or different to that of the Bible, they have a decision to make. This decision identifies their honesty. When an honest person learns their faith, worship, religion, or doctrine is inconsistent with the Bible, they will repent and conform to the truth. The dishonest person does not change his course, but seeks to justify himself.

Some today imitate those in Athens in the first century. *"For all the Athenians and the foreigners who were there spent their time in nothing else but either to tell or to hear some new thing" (Acts 17:21)*. This attitude can only result in division. Those who introduce something "new" in the religion of Christ and declare it pleases God, or that it originated from God are false teachers. There can be no doubt why Paul informed the Roman Christians of the following, *"Now I urge you, brethren, note those who cause divisions and offenses, contrary to the doctrine which you learned, and avoid them" (Rom. 16:17)*. One reason is, the person introducing a new doctrine divides God's people and themselves from being unified with God.

Conclusion

God's revealed standard, the gospel, is changeless. Religious division among men is inevitable when they author a change to it, or author another doctrine. Only the word of God achieves the result He and man both desire—salvation. The Bible is replete with examples of those who deviated from God's word and suffered the fierceness of His anger. The Father and Son say what they mean, and mean what they say. We cannot tell them what they want or desire. We can only know what that is from what they have revealed.

Questions and Discussion

1. What is the core reason for religious division?

2. In John 17, Jesus prayed for the unity of believers. What example of unity does He offer?

3. In what way are the Father and Son "one?"

4. From John 17:9-17, what does Jesus pray that the basis for the unity of believers should be?

5. What promise does Jesus make to His disciples that ensures they will remember the information He wants to impart to the world?

6. Jesus quoted Isaiah in Mathew 15:8-9. What inevitable conclusion must be drawn?

7. Read 1 Cor. 1:10, 4:17, 7:17, and 16:1. From these verses, what is Paul reinforcing to this divided congregation?

8. What conclusion does Jesus' reply to the chief priests, scribes, and elders force us to make (Mark 11:27-30)?

9. How can we be sure we are investing our faith in what God wants?

10. Review Gal. 1:6-10. For what sin did Paul rebuke the Galatians, and what word emphasizes its seriousness?

11. How should the responsible person approach any subject concerning religion (1 Thes. 5:21-22; Rom. 12:2)?

The Anatomy of Unity and Division

Lesson Five

Attitudes and Motives That Cause Division

A statement I heard many years ago was, "Everyone does everything they do for a reason." Nothing is truer when it comes to the motives of those who cause religious division. In some cases, their motive is obvious. However, many times the motive is camouflaged behind a mask of "so-called" religious sincerity and zeal. It is usually only a matter of time before this mask is seen through, and the true motive is exposed. Religious division always has sin involved on the part of one or both parties. This lesson is designed to understand the motives behind those who incite, aid, or abet division that is not based on a Biblical principle or sin. Lesson Eight will explore the only scriptural basis for division.

1. Base gain.

The KJV uses the term *"filthy lucre,"* and the NKJV translates this as *"covetousness."* Of all places one would hope a sinful desire for gain would not be found, is in the church. However, from its earliest days, men have used Jesus' church in sinful ways to better their personal financial situation. The inspired writers of the N.T. did not shrink back from warning of this possibility, identifying the perpetrators and exposing their motives.

In Paul's list of qualification for elders and deacons, he uses the phrase, *"not greedy for money" (1 Tim. 3:3, 8 and Titus 1:7)*. Peter's warning is similar when describing the character of men who shepherd the flock when he writes, *"serving as overseers, not by compulsion but willingly, not for dishonest gain but eagerly" (1 Pet. 5:2)*. Men who have oversight of the financial affairs of the congregation can be subjected to the temptation to misappropriate funds to themselves. A man who has demonstrated this character flaw should never be appointed to serve as a leader in Christ's church. When covetous leaders or members are found taking financial advantage of the church or its members, and the matter is not dealt with, the congregation will be polarized, and division is inevitable.

2. Pride, Stubbornness, and Arrogance.

Few things bring out the worst in people and divide brethren, friends, and family like the attitudes of pride, stubbornness, and arrogance. Unlike base gain, one, if not all three, sins are present when a congregation divides over matters of judgment. When someone dogmatically insists on having their way, thinks they are more enlightened than others, or stubbornly refuses to come to terms of agreement, division is foreseeable. And if not, it ruptures friendships, strains relationships, and undermines the trust so desperately needed for the congregation to function at its full potential. Working with this kind of person challenges others to maintain self-control and makes them want to draw back to keep from being subjected to confrontation. The Bible repeatedly condemns this behavior for at least two obvious reasons: 1. It divides God's people. 2. It separates the person who commits these sins from God.

Peter and James reminded their readers that *"God resists the proud and gives grace to the humble" (James 4:6; 1 Pet. 5:5)*. When Samuel told Saul that God was rejecting him as king, he said, "rebellion is as the sin of witchcraft, and stubborness is as iniquity and idolatry" (1 Sam. 15:23).

The difference between pride and humility is pride seeks glory, humility receives glory.

Paul stated the recipe that always results in unity, peace, and harmony when he wrote, *"Let nothing be done through selfish ambition or conceit, but in lowliness of mind let each esteem others better than himself. Let each of you look out not only for his own interests, but also for the interests of others" (Phil. 2:3-4)*. Pride and arrogance are self-serving and the antithesis of Christianity.

The Savior's example serves as our pattern for meekness, humility, and servitude. *"But made Himself of no reputation, taking the form of a bondservant, and coming in the likeness of men. And being found in appearance as a man, He humbled Himself and became obedient to the point of death, even the death of the cross" (Phil. 2:7-8)*. Jesus was in the likeness of men, walked with men, yet was the epitome of humility. He repeatedly prayed, *"not My will but Your will be done."* He did not call attention to Himself, though His teaching, servitude, and humility drew a crowd. The difference between pride and humility is pride seeks glory, humility receives glory.

"Arrogance" means "pomp, pride and swelling" (Strongs). It is demonstrated by braggadocio or boasting. It elevates oneself at the expense of another, and blackens others to whitewash themselves. The Proverb writer states, *"The fear of the Lord is to hate evil; pride and arrogance and the evil way and the perverse mouth I hate" (Prov. 8:13).* James rebuked those to whom he wrote for their selfish and boastful estimation of themselves and failing to recognize God as being responsible for their blessings. *"Whereas you do not know what will happen tomorrow. For what is your life? It is even a vapor that appears for a little time and then vanishes away. Instead, you ought to say, 'If the Lord wills, we shall live and do this or that.' But now you boast in your arrogance. All such boasting is evil"* (James 4:14-16).

Conclusion

Let us be reminded again, the list of seven things the Lord God hates begins with *"a proud look"* and ends with *"he that sows discord among brethren" (Prov. 6:16-19).* It is not a coincidence that one sin leads to another. The pride, arrogance, and stubbornness that divides congregations will neither go unnoticed nor unpunished on the Judgment Day. Motives may remain hidden from men, but the Great Judge will expose them.

Questions and Discussion

1. How can base gain, or the love of money, cause division in the church?

2. Read 1 Tim. 3:3, 8; Titus 1:7; and 1 Pet. 5:2. Why did the inspired writers command that those greedy of gain were unqualified to be leaders in the church?

3. Define the terms pride, arrogance, and stubbornness. How are these attitudes and motives manifested?

The Anatomy of Unity and Division

4. What is the difference between pride and humility?

5. Discuss Samuel's indictment of King Saul in 1 Sam. 15:23, and the results.

6. What usually results in relationships when pride, arrogance, or stubbornness are exhibited?

7. What word occurs in the scriptures that Paul and Peter quote describing God's attitude toward these character traits?

8. How does James rebuke his readers for attributing their plans and success to themselves?

9. How does Phil. 3:3-4 equip us to avoid division in the church that results from pride, arrogance, and stubbornness?

10. Explain why Jesus is the perfect pattern of humility that we must imitate.

11. Read Prov. 6:16-19. Discuss the connection between "a proud look" and "he who sows discord among brethren."

Lesson Six

Methods Employed That Cause Division

Though Paul stated that we are not ignorant of Satan's devices in 2 Corinthians 2:11, yet many Christians are. Again, this lesson is dealing with rancorous division in the church over matters of judgment. All divisions of this sort are inherently evil. The fountainhead of all division is Satan, and he accomplishes his mission through the methods men employ. Satan's goal is to undermine all that is good for man from God and destroy the souls of believers. This lesson seeks to expose some of the methods employed by men to divide God's people.

1. Lies and Deception.

Those who used deceptive means to divide God's people in Jesus' day are no different than those who do so today. Of this sort, Jesus said, *"You are of your father the devil, and the desires of your father you want to do. He was a murderer from the beginning, and does not stand in the truth, because there is no truth in him. When he speaks a lie, he speaks from his own resources, for he is a liar and the father of it" (John 8:44)*. To lie, deceive, or repeat falsehood to rupture a congregation is to play into the devil's hand as his child. Deceptive Christians will stop at nothing to achieve their desired results. Many good elders, preachers, and members of the Lord's church have been misrepresented, resulting in the polarization of a congregation. Satan's servants used this very same method to condemn and crucify Jesus.

The reason lies and deception must be used to make good men look bad and divide the church is because, the truth about good men has no power to indict. Only the lies forged by some, and believed by others, sow seeds of doubt and division. *"The words of a talebearer are like tasty trifles, and they go down into the inmost body" (Prov. 18:8)*. We need to be reminded that God hates *"a lying tongue"* and *"he who bears false witness" (Prov. 6:16-19)*. The Proverb writer says many things about the misuse of the tongue and spreading misinformation. These include, *"An ungodly man digs up evil, and it is on his lips like a burning fire. A perverse man sows strife, and a whisperer separates the best of friends" (Prov. 16:27-28)*.

The lies and deception the devil's servants use eventually takes the form of slander. In Greek, slander is nearly letter for letter our English word "blaspheme." The speaking evil of Christians that divides congregations comes from a heart filled with evil. Jesus said, *"A good man out of the good treasure of his heart brings forth good; and an evil man out of the evil treasure of his heart brings forth evil. For out of the abundance of the heart his mouth speaks" (Luke 6:45).* Slander is a trademark of the devil and the hypocrite, *"The hypocrite with his mouth destroys his neighbor" (Prov. 11:9).*

Not only is division sparked by lies and deception, but the person who keeps spreading the tales is fanning its flames. *"Where there is no wood, the fire goes out; And where there is no talebearer, strife ceases" (Prov. 26:20).* The speed at which information is communicated today has contributed much good, but perhaps as much evil. The gospel can go

> **Envy, or self-seeking, is always at the expense of another and drives in a wedge of division.**

around the world in seconds, and brethren can spread their divisive lies, deception, and slander equally as fast. Cell phones, texting, the internet, and email are only a few methods used to share a divisive Christian's agenda. Some Christians have been known to embark on an all-out electronic campaign to rally support for their divisive cause.

This type of communication begs the question, "What should the faithful Christian's attitude and response be to those who distribute divisive dialogue?" Paul told Titus what was needed when misinformation was being disseminated. *"For there are many insubordinate, both idle talkers and deceivers, especially those of the circumcision, whose mouths must be stopped, who subvert whole households, teaching things which they ought not, for the sake of dishonest gain" (Titus 1:10-11).* Their mouths can be stopped by refusing to entertain their divisive speech. When you refuse to listen, speaking stops. In addition to refusing to listen, they need to be warned of the retribution awaiting them.

2. Secret Meetings.

The leaders of division always know who they should avoid with their divisive schemes and who will listen to them. Using whatever media of communication is convenient, they arrange a meeting(s). These meetings are where they spread their lies and slander to create a campaign that recruits followers. Paul exposes this method to the Galatians when he wrote, *"And this occurred because of false brethren secretly brought in (who came in by stealth to spy out our liberty which we have in Christ Jesus, that they might bring us into bondage), to whom we did not yield submission even for an hour, that the truth of the gospel might continue with you" (Gal. 2:4-5).* These secret methods were used to teach false doctrine. However, the same method is used today to recruit support for someone's opinion and personal agenda. Paul turned these men away because they were promoting something the gospel did not. We must take the same stand and never give audience to someone trying to polarize the church. Paul reveals how to react to the person promoting division, what their motive is, and the character of those they prey upon. *"Now I urge you, brethren, note those who cause divisions and offenses, contrary to the doctrine which you learned, and avoid them. For those who are such do not serve our Lord Jesus Christ, but their own belly, and by smooth words and flattering speech deceive the hearts of the simple" (Rom. 16:17-18).*

Secrecy is the opposite of how Jesus conducted all His affairs. When on trial before Pilate, He declared, *"I spoke openly to the world. I always taught in synagogues and in the temple, where the Jews always meet, and in secret I have said nothing" (John 18:20).* Brethren approaching others in secret have a hidden agenda that is inconsistent with the example of Jesus and His word, and the preservation of unity. The faithful Christian must learn to deflect this device of the devil and remember the words of Solomon, *"For God will bring every work into judgment, including every secret thing, whether good or evil" (Eccl. 12:14).*

Conclusion

Paul uses the words *"envy"* and *"strife"* to describe the worldliness of the Corinthians. *"For you are still carnal. For where there are envy, strife, and divisions among you, are you not carnal and behaving like mere men?" (1 Cor. 3:3-4).* These self-promoting character traits are a core reason why so many issues are allowed to cause division. These two evils are markers for even more sin. **"For where envy and self-seeking exist, confusion** *and every evil thing are there" (Jas. 3:16-17).* Envy, or self-seeking, is always at the expense of another and drives in a wedge of division.

Questions and Discussion

1. Where does division in the church originate?

2. Who is the spiritual father of those spreading lies and deception for their agenda?

3. From Proverbs 16:27-28, list the traits mentioned therein and their results.

4. Where do good or evil thoughts and speech originate from a man (Luke 6:45)?

5. What is the application of, "Where there is no wood, the fire goes out; And where there is no talebearer, strife ceases" (Prov. 26:20)?

6. What should be your response to those who attempt to spread misinformation?

7. What is another word for "slander" and what does it mean?

8. What was the method used by some to infiltrate the Galatians?

9. Why would someone have a secret meeting with a select few members of the congregation?

10. What was the motive of those inciting division among the Christians that Paul exposed to the Romans, and what action did he command them to take?

11. What else is present with envy or self-seeking?

12. After reading Ecc. 12:14 and Matt. 12:36, what should be our attitude towards communicating information that could cause division?

The Anatomy of Unity and Division

Lesson Seven

The Collateral Damage of Religious Division

Cause and effect are not limited to the physical realm, but are easily observed in the spiritual realm. We have thus far studied some of the causes of religious division and shall, in this lesson, explore some of its collateral damage. The ultimate result of religious division for some can be summed up in two words—eternal condemnation. However, experience and the Bible have taught this author that there are other results on this side of eternity. While Christians believe in eternal condemnation, it isn't easy to comprehend from our earthly vista. On the other hand, damage inflicted by the sin of division in the church is clearly visible. Let us be reminded that this lesson considers the results of division in matters of judgment and expediency.

1. Destroys Friendships.

Religious division can create conflict in nearly all human relationships, perhaps no more so than with fellow members of the church. Brethren who were friends, worked, and worshipped together, have been known to sever ties and refuse to speak to one another after enduring division. For some, rupture in the church is promoted with bitter words and caustic attitudes aimed at friends. These offensive sins are locked in the memory of the offended, and no amount of pleading for forgiveness will unlock them. *"A brother offended is harder to win than a strong city, and contentions are like the bars of a castle" (Prov. 18:19)*. When brethren refuse to extend kindness and courtesy when differences arise, feelings are hurt, sides are chosen, and the divide widens. *"Can two walk together, unless they are agreed?" (Amos 3:3)*. The obvious answer is, "no."

In many cases, it is not always the subject of the disagreement that causes the most distress, but rather the attitude and speech used when discussing it. *"A soft answer turns away wrath, but a harsh word stirs up anger" (Prov. 15:1)*. Loud or harsh speech can put others on the defensive because they are made to feel as though they are defending themselves from an attack. When approached with meekness and humility, differences can be discussed and amicable resolutions will result, Paul wrote, *"Let your speech always be with grace, seasoned with salt, that you may know how you ought to answer each one" (Col. 4:6)*.

The Anatomy of Unity and Division

2. Thwarts The Cause of Christ.

Jesus said, *"A new commandment I give to you, that you love one another; as I have loved you, that you also love one another. By this all will know that you are My disciples, if you have love for one another"* (John 13:34-35). Those outside the church usually have a good concept of how Christians should treat one another. In fact, when the world sees Christians unified and demonstrating brotherly love, it is appealing. On the other hand, when they see rancor, bitterness, and division, they want no part of it. Their attitudes are, "I have all the bitterness and division I need without church." Or, "if those people in the church cannot get along, why do I want to join their ranks?" Or, "I am just as good as they are." While there is no good reason for not becoming or being a member of the church, it provides a handle some believe is worth holding on to.

> **In many cases, it is not always the subject of the disagreement that causes the most distress, but rather the attitude and speech used when discussing it. "A soft answer turns away wrath, but a harsh word stirs up anger" (Prov. 15:1).**

The church was designed and built by Jesus as a place where its members could expect love, kindness, and unity to prevail among its members. However, when members focus on warring with one another, the cause Jesus designed His church to promote comes to a halt. This is precisely why the devil incites division, and his servants in the church cause it. Paul's letter to the Romans identifies the hypocrisy of the Jews claiming to live by the moral and religious code of God's Law, yet they violated it in every way. This hypocrisy did not go unnoticed by the Gentiles. *"You who make your boast in the law, do you dishonor God through breaking the law? For the name of God is blasphemed among the Gentiles because of you, as it is written"* (Rom. 2:23-24). The outsider knows evil is present when Christians making their boast in the Law of Christ, and claiming to serve the Prince of Peace are divided. When this occurs, the church is laughed to scorn and her influence and reputation can take years to rebuild. Paul accurately defines where division leads when writing, *"For all the law is fulfilled in one word, even in this: "You shall love your neighbor as yourself." But if you bite and devour one another, beware lest you be consumed by one another!" (Gal. 5:14-15).* Brotherly love is always absent on the part of some when division in the church occurs.

3. Some Fall Away and Become Unfaithful.

In nearly every case of division in the Lord's church, there are spiritual casualties. Some who cannot be influenced by either party in the division, just "give up." When they see the evil behavior of Christians, especially those they have respected, they say, "Why bother?" And as mentioned in point number 1 of this lesson, they may have been deeply hurt. There is no justifiable reason for casting away our faith in Jesus or severing fellowship with the church. However, many have severed their ties with the religion of Christ because of division over matters of judgment.

Jesus mentions those who fall away in the parable of the sower and soils. *"But the ones on the rock are those who, when they hear, receive the word with joy; and these have no root, who believe for a while and in time of temptation fall away" (Luke 8:13).* Sadly, the temptation to sever ties altogether with the church is given in to by those whose spirituality is shallow. The person who believes fulfillment is found in others will be disappointed sooner or later. When one places absolute trust and confidence in God, their faith will enable them to overcome every obstacle, including division in the church. Failing to have the "seek first" mentality makes it easy to give up and defect from the Lord's cause. *"The backslider in heart will be filled with his own ways, but a good man will be satisfied from above" (Prov. 14:14).*

Conclusion

While division in the church is evil and heartbreaking, we need to think about the resolve first-century Christians had to have to be faithful. Paul asks the rhetorical question, *"Who shall separate us from the love of Christ? Shall tribulation, or distress, or persecution, or famine, or nakedness, or peril, or sword? As it is written: 'For Your sake we are killed all day long; We are accounted as sheep for the slaughter.' Yet in all these things we are more than conquerors through Him who loved us. For I am persuaded that neither death nor life, nor angels nor principalities nor powers, nor things present nor things to come, nor height nor depth, nor any other created thing, shall be able to separate us from the love of God which is in Christ Jesus our Lord" (Rom. 8:35-39).*

Questions and Discussion

1. What are the causes of severed relationships among Christians when there are disagreements in the church over matters of judgment or expediencies?

2. Read Prov. 18:19. Why is it so difficult to be reconciled with an offended brother?

3. Why do issues that could be resolved easily, escalate into division in the church?

4. Differences of opinion will always arise in matters of judgment and expediency. Read John 13:34 and Col. 4:6 and explain how applying these verses to disagreements will result in unity.

5. Of what do those outside the church usually have a general idea about division?

6. Why does religious division thwart the cause of Christ, and how do non-Christians reply when they observe division?

7. List the things that Jesus designed and built the church for that should make it appealing.

8. What was the result of the Jews' hypocrisy when keeping the law of Moses (Rom. 2:23-24)?

9. What words did Paul use to describe the religious division of the Galatians (Gal. 5:14-15)?

10. What are some reasons Christians fall away, or defect from the church when division is present? And, what is their core reason? (Luke 8:13, Prov. 14:14)?

11. Read Heb. 6:4-6. Discuss the things listed that the backslider forfeits and why "it is impossible to renew them again to repentance."

12. After considering Rom. 8:35-39, discuss the endurance of first-century Christians and compare their struggles to remain faithful with the reasons brethren divide or become unfaithful today.

The Anatomy of Unity and Division

Lesson Eight

The Only Justifiable Cause for Religious Division

The design of this lesson series focuses on religious division over matters of opinion and expediency. Division for these reasons angers God and His Son, who died to purchase the church. However, it is important to recognize religious division often arises when perpetrators introduce false doctrine and refuse to repent when admonished. In some cases, it takes the form of introducing something that profanes worship. Another strategy is the endorsement and tolerance of immorality by leadership, preaching, or teaching, or any other way used to disagree with the standard of the New Testament (NT).

False teachers generally sanction something men want and God either forbids or of which He is silent. Paul wrote to Timothy, *"For the time will come when they will not endure sound doctrine, but according to their own desires, because they have itching ears, they will heap up for themselves teachers; and they will turn their ears away from the truth, and be turned aside to fables" (2 Tim. 4:3-4).* Clauses like, *"their own desires," "itching ears,"* and *"heap up teachers for themselves"* describe the motives of false teachers. There are always those eager to listen and accept something outside of the truth. These include false doctrine regarding adultery, homosexuality, divorce and remarriage for any cause, the use of mechanical instruments in worship, grace, the financial support of human institutions from the church treasury, the 70 AD doctrine, women preachers, abortion, and the list seems to grow with each generation.

Isaiah warned the people of God about the false influences of their day. Paul quotes one of his warnings, *"Come out from among them and be separate, says the Lord" (2 Cor. 6:17).* Paul's reason for stating this is obvious when one familiarizes themselves with his letters to the Corinthians. They were being bombarded with doctrines contrary to the N.T. because they originated with men. Jesus equated the commandments and doctrine of men with vain worship. *"And in vain they worship Me, teaching as doctrines the commandments of men" (Matt. 15:9).* When a faithful Christian discovers they are working and worshipping with a congregation that is operating based on man-made doctrine, they have no choice but to remove themselves, else their worship is in vain. Paul echoes Jesus' sentiments in Rom. 16:17-18, *"Now I urge you, brethren, note those who cause divisions and offenses, contrary to the doctrine* which you learned, and avoid them. For those who are such do not serve our Lord Jesus Christ, but their own belly, and by smooth words and flattering speech deceive the hearts of the simple." "Note" ("mark" KJV) and "avoid" are unmistakable terms that should describe the faithful Christian's attitude and action when false doctrine is present. Unfortunately, this occurs in the church, and sometimes, few if any members take the commanded action. Jesus, nor His inspired authors, make a distinction regarding "who" the false teacher is. When a brother in the church is propagating false doctrine, the command is, *"note and avoid,"* regardless of the consensus of others. Every doctrine either originates with God or men (Matt. 21:25).

Accomplices to false teachers include those who fail to take a stand against them and their false teachings.

Paul charged the Thessalonians, *"But we command you, brethren, in the name of our Lord Jesus Christ, that you withdraw from every brother who walks disorderly and not according to the tradition which he received from us"* (2 Thess. 3:6). It is the responsibility of elders to guard the flock and lead them in withdrawing from a false teacher. Unfortunately, some elders either lack the knowledge, the courage, or believe they should not carry out this command. When leadership abdicates its God-given responsibility to combat false doctrine and its teachers, the individual must act. They must separate themselves from this evil influence.

Accomplices to false teachers include those who fail to take a stand against them and their false teachings. *"Whoever transgresses and does not abide in the doctrine of Christ does not have God. He who abides in the doctrine of Christ has both the Father and the Son. If anyone comes to you and does not bring this doctrine, do not receive him into your house nor greet him; for he who greets him shares in his evil deeds"* (2 John 9-11). It is no secret that some congregations of the church of Christ teach or tolerate false doctrine. Sadly, some of their members know it and refuse to separate themselves. The accomplice will not be spared in the judgment. Without an audience, the false teacher and his doctrine wither away. But if some stand with him, he will thrive.

When division occurs among brethren over matters of judgment and expediency, someone has sinned. Separating ourselves from false teachers is commanded because their doctrine is sinful. The Christian must reflect the attitude Paul commands, *"Test all things; hold fast what is good. Abstain from every form of evil" (1 Thess. 5:21-21)*. When a doctrine fails to meet the test and scrutiny of the NT, Christians must avoid it at all costs. John wrote, *"Beloved, do not believe every spirit, but test the spirits, whether they are of God; because many false prophets have gone out into the world" (1 John 4:1)*. John's warning to his readers was no doubt because there were men claiming to be prophets of God, who were not inspired by the Holy Spirit as the genuine Prophets were. They were commanded to "test." In our culture, it is considered unpopular to question or challenge a man who claims to be teaching and preaching God's word. However, Paul and John taught us to do so. Any man who refuses to have his teaching put to the "test" of the NT probably has something to hide.

Paul gave an unequivocal command and exposed the motive of the false teacher to Timothy, along with his reaction—*"withdraw yourself." "If anyone teaches otherwise and does not consent to wholesome words, even the words of our Lord Jesus Christ, and to the doctrine which accords with godliness, he is proud, knowing nothing, but is obsessed with disputes and arguments over words, from which come envy, strife, reviling, evil suspicions, useless wranglings of men of corrupt minds and destitute of the truth, who suppose that godliness is a means of gain. From such withdraw yourself" (1 Tim. 6:3-5)*. Whether the congregation withdraws from the false teacher, or the individual does, pulling away from brethren you know and love is very difficult. However, God commands it for our good and theirs. *"And if anyone does not obey our word in this epistle, note that person and do not keep company with him, that he may be ashamed. Yet do not count him as an enemy, but admonish him as a brother" (2 Thess. 3:14-15)*. Hopefully, the disobedient person will recognize that the severed relationship and lost social ties will cause two things. 1. They will be ashamed. 2. They will realize they are forfeiting their relationship with the Heavenly Father.

Conclusion

Religious division always involves sin, whether overt and obvious or lurking beneath the surface. Regardless of the form it takes, something must be done. When false teachers refuse to abide by the doctrine of the N.T., elders should remove them from their duty, and any who aid and abet. If they refuse to do this, the faithful Christian must remove himself from the source. Remember the words of Paul, *"You ran well. Who hindered you from obeying the truth? This persuasion does not come from Him who calls you. A little leaven leavens the whole lump"* (Gal. 5:7-9).

Questions and Discussion

1. What do false teachers usually offer their audience?

2. What does 2 Tim. 4:3-4 reveal about the motives of the false teacher?

3. What statement does Paul quote from Isaiah that tells us what our responsibility is?

4. What does Jesus say is the result of teaching for doctrine the commandments of men?

5. How does Jesus' question in Matt. 21:25 address the two sources of religious doctrine?

6. What is the responsibility of elders to the congregation when false doctrine is taught. (Rom. 16:17-18, 2 Thess. 3:6)

7. Why do some elders refuse to lead the congregation in disfellowshipping a false teacher or unruly members?

8. What should be the individual's response when leadership endorses or tolerates false teaching with no intention of effecting a change?

9. How can a person be an accomplice to false teachers and false doctrine?

10. Why did the Apostles Paul and John use the words "test" and "try" when writing to Christians? And what is used to make the final decision based on these examinations?

11. What is always present when religious division occurs?

12. How does "a little leaven leavens the whole lump apply to this study?

The Anatomy of Unity and Division

Lesson Nine

The Scriptural Solution for Division

Yes, religious division can be resolved, whether it concerns matters of judgment, expediency, or even doctrine. Unity can only result and be sustained when all involved submit to the will of God. Unfortunately, how to heal the breach is rarely discussed; only unhealthy communication that causes separation is communicated. In fact, what should be the first topic of discussion—unity and how it can be achieved—is never considered. When the "party spirit" prevails in matters of judgment or expediency, a faction begins planning an exodus, securing a place to meet, and drawing away members to their cause. This "party spirit" is sinful.

This lesson examines what the Bible demands of Christians that will always unify. And, if they had been present to begin with, division would not have occurred. When all concerned apply the virtues Jesus demands found in sacred truth, division will dissolve. The absence of any of these virtues invariably leads to unnecessary tension or division.

1. Brotherly Love.

Love is the foundation of all that is good. The lack of love is always at the core of division. Man is incapable of defining love; only God can because He is love (1 John 4:8). And He does not only "claim" to love, He demonstrated it. His example is our pattern for defining our character, speech, and actions. *"And walk in love, as Christ also has loved us and given Himself for us, an offering and a sacrifice to God for a sweet-smelling aroma"* (Eph. 5:2). When we are defined as the kind of person that loves like God, unity cannot help but prevail.

When Christians, congregations, marriages or families are divided, love is missing on the part of one or both parties. Sin is always present in the absence of love. Jesus said, *"If you love Me, keep My commandments"* (John 14:15). If we do not obey His commandments, we do not love Him. If we love Him, we will allow nothing to stand in our way of obeying Him. When we love our brethren, we will allow nothing on our part that promotes division.

The love demanded by God is described by *"Let love be without hypocrisy. Abhor what is evil. Cling to what is good. Be kindly affectionate to one another with brotherly love, in honor giving preference to one another"* (Rom. 12:9-10). The preferential treatment of others exhibits brotherly love. Mistreatment of others demonstrates a lack of love, is self-serving, and causes division. One either loves their brother or does not. Paul identifies the debt that all have, which is never satisfied. And, when everyone continues making installments on it, there will be no division. *"Owe no one anything except to love one another, for he who loves another has fulfilled the law"* (Rom. 13:8). When brethren are not unified, someone is not making the payments. A similar thought is shared in 1 Cor. 12:25, *"that there should be no schism in the body, but that the members should have the same care for one another."*

> **When working through disagreements, patience or longsuffering cannot be overemphasized. In most cases, problems did not arise overnight, and an amicable resolution may take time.**

The church at Corinth was divided over several issues. Paul's treatise on love in 1 Cor. 13 was central to eliminating their problems and stimulating unity. He describes what love is and what it is not. He begins love's definition with, *"Though I speak with the tongues of men and of angels, but have not love, I have become sounding brass or a clanging cymbal. And though I have the gift of prophecy, and understand all mysteries and all knowledge, and though I have all faith, so that I could remove mountains, but have not love, I am nothing. And though I bestow all my goods to feed the poor, and though I give my body to be burned, but have not love, it profits me nothing"* (1 Cor. 13:1-3). The Christian who does not have love, regardless of their achievements or their gifts, is "nothing" without love. They are spiritually bankrupt and void of the fundamental characteristic of God that they should imitate. Why? Because God created us in His image, and God is love. We should be imitating Him.

2. Humility.

This virtue sets the stage for healing division in all areas of life. Its absence causes friction. Pride, the opposite of humility, stresses any relationship where it raises its sinful head. When divided parties come to the table with humility, resolution will result. When one or both parties refuse to be humble, the wedge cannot be removed, only driven deeper.

Humility is mentioned many times in the Bible. However, the consequences of pride speak volumes to the problem of division. *"By pride comes nothing but strife, but with the well-advised is wisdom"* (Prov. 13:10). "Pride" in this text means "arrogance." The strife that results from pride fans the embers that turn into the flames of division. Paul states one of the best recipes for unity, *"Let nothing be done through selfish ambition or conceit, but in lowliness of mind let each esteem others better than himself. Let each of you look out not only for his own interests, but also for the interests of others"* (Phil. 2:3-4). When everyone *"esteems the other better than himself,"* the friction is quenched. Jesus was undeniably others oriented. His disciples who are not others-oriented are not pleasing Him. Peter states the need for humility and compares it to a garment that is to be worn by the faithful. *"Likewise, you younger people, submit yourselves to your elders. Yes, all of you be submissive to one another, and be clothed with humility, for "God resists the proud, but gives grace to the humble"* (1 Pet. 5:5). The robe of humility is beautiful, the rags of pride are ugly, sinful, and divisive.

3. Kindness.

Sadly, kindness seems to be a fading virtue in our culture. Among other qualities that should characterize Christians and ensure unity, Paul commands kindness. *"Therefore, as the elect of God, holy and beloved, put on tender mercies, kindness, humility, meekness, longsuffering; bearing with one another, and forgiving one another"* (Col. 3:12-13). Strongs defines "kindness" in this text as, "moral excellence in character or demeanor," and it is also translated as gentleness. When divided parties approach one another with kindness and humility, another foundation stone is laid for establishing unity. What do you think Jesus' reaction would be to someone who disagreed with Him, if they approached Him kindly? Paul reminds the Ephesians of the divine example of kindness when he wrote, *"And be kind to one another, tenderhearted, forgiving one another, even as God in Christ forgave you"* (Eph. 4:32).

Few things demonstrate kindness like our speech. When one reflects kindness in their discussions, they remove a key factor that contributes to division. *"A soft answer turns away wrath, but a harsh word stirs up anger"* (Prov. 15:1). A sure way to excite the ire in others is by raising your voice or using harsh, unkind speech. It pushes others away rather than drawing them closer. As we understand the preservative nature of salt, perhaps this is why Paul wrote, *"Let your speech always be with grace, seasoned with salt, that you may know how you ought to answer each one" (Col. 4:6).* Kindness in speech will unify divided parties and preserve relationships, rather than widen the divide.

4. Longsuffering.

When working through disagreements, patience or longsuffering cannot be overemphasized. In most cases, problems did not arise overnight, and an amicable resolution may take time. When we turn the word "longsuffering" around, we have "suffer long." Unity is priceless and worth suffering for, though the actions and attitudes of some Christians devalue it. The Greek word for longsuffering is "makrothumia" i.e., "forbearance, or subjectively fortitude." (Vines) It is the idea of not heating up too quickly. Another of Paul's list of character traits that the Christian must possess includes longsuffering, *"But the fruit of the Spirit is love, joy, peace, longsuffering, kindness, goodness, faithfulness, gentleness, self-control" (Gal. 5:22-23).* All of these qualities are needed to heal division and preserve unity.

> **To forgive others as God does means you let the offense go and refuse to revisit it.**

When a Christian understands they are to imitate the Father and the Son to please them, they will mimic their example of longsuffering. And, when they do, unity can be restored where ties have been severed. It was the longsuffering of God that made it possible for man to be united with Him. *"The Lord is not slack concerning His promise, as some count slackness, but is longsuffering toward us, not willing that any should perish but that all should come to repentance" (2 Pet. 3:9).* It may just be that your longsuffering with others will make unity with them possible.

5. Forgiveness.

When brethren are divided and measures are being taken to reunite them, forgiveness must take place wherever it is needed. The Father and Son are the primary examples to consider when defining forgiveness, as with all other qualities of godliness.

The Psalmist praises the nature and extent of God's forgiveness when he writes, *"For as the heavens are high above the earth, so great is His mercy toward those who fear Him; As far as the east is from the west, so far has He removed our transgressions from us"* (Psa. 103:11-12). When Isaiah pleaded with God's people to repent, he quotes the Father's willingness to forgive and the completeness of it. *"I, even I, am He who blots out your transgressions for My own sake; And I will not remember your sins"* (Isa. 43:25). To forgive others as God does means you let the offense go and refuse to revisit it.

When Peter suggests to Jesus that he should forgive others seven times, Jesus said, *"I do not say to you, up to seven times, but up to seventy times seven"* (Matt. 18:22). In essence, forgiveness must be limitless, because God's is. And to bring our understanding of the importance of forgiving others, we need to be reminded of Jesus' words, *"For if you forgive men their trespasses, your heavenly Father will also forgive you. But if you do not forgive men their trespasses, neither will your Father forgive your trespasses"* (Matt. 6:14-15). Some may think they do not have to forgive. And, they are correct if they want to forfeit God's forgiveness.

When true forgiveness is extended, the past will remain just that, in the past. When old wounds are reopened, division will result. Jesus does not remember the sins we committed that nailed Him to the cross when we have met the terms of forgiveness. Neither should we hold others hostage with the sins they have committed against us, which were forgiven. Extending forgiveness is not always easy, but without it, the wounds of division cannot heal. Paul shares the command and the example of forgiveness in this brief statement. *"Bearing with one another, and forgiving one another, if anyone has a complaint against another; even as Christ"* (Col. 3:13).

Conclusion

Every good virtue must be present in all parties for unity to be restored among divided brethren. We could study several others from the inspired writers. The absence, neglect, or lackluster efforts to employ and guard any make unity difficult, if not impossible. Any substitute for these qualities, cannot produce the same results. Paul sets forth a list of traits that should define the life of a Christian just before telling them *"to keep the unity of the Spirit,"* when he wrote, *"I, therefore, the prisoner of the Lord, beseech you to walk worthy of the calling with which you were called, with all lowliness and gentleness, with longsuffering, bearing with one another in love, endeavoring to keep the unity of the Spirit in the bond of peace" (Eph. 4:1-3).* The word "bond" could be translated "band." This word picture might be illustrated with the metal bands on a barrel that keep the staves in place to serve the vessel's purpose. The virtues demanded by Jesus are what keep His people together and enable them serve His purpose with maximum potential.

Questions and Discussion

1. How have the Father and Son demonstrated their love, and how can we imitate their example?

2. What virtue is always absent in Christians, friends, or a congregation when there is division?

3. Define and discuss each of the qualities mentioned in Rom. 12:9-10 that help heal division and secure unity.

4. What is the debt all Christians owe one another?

5. Review the imagery and word pictures in 1 Cor. 13:1-3 that Paul uses to introduce the definition of love. How is the person described who does not have love?

6. What is the difference between pride and humility?

7. What results in relationships when pride exists?

8. Review each character trait in Phil. 2:3-4. How does the application of each prevent or remedy division?

9. What is God's attitude and reaction to pride? To humility?

10. What is longsuffering, and why is it important to restoring and preserving unity?

11. How did God demonstrate longsuffering, and what is the result of it?

12. Why is longsuffering so important to healing and or preventing division?

13. Is forgiveness optional? Explain your answer?

14. Why must all parties have forgiveness for unity to be restored and preserved?

15. What is the consequence for those who desire forgiveness but refuse to forgive?

16. Where is a command and example offered in scripture for forgiveness?

Lesson Ten

The Preservation of Congregational Unity

For those who have endured division in the church, the preservation of unity is of supreme importance. Preserving unity should be, and must be, the objective of every Christian. And when it is, it will eliminate the possibility for Satan's fiery darts and wedges of division to be effective.

1. Beware, On Guard, and Alert.

When brethren think division cannot happen, or they ignore early warning signs, the dreaded result is predictable. The Bible uses the word "body" to describe the relationship of members to one another, and the members' relationship to the Head, which is Christ. When problems arise in the body (church), the Head is never the source, but always with its members.

The NT is replete with warnings about various threats to the church. All of which have the potential to cause division. Some of these warnings are regarding actions and attitudes about matters of judgment or expediency, and others are about matters of doctrine. In all cases, when friction is present or division results, the same actions and attitudes are present. The presence of these actions and attitudes is why the inspired writers command that we beware and be alert.

Following Peter's warning to his readers that untaught and unstable teachers would twist the scriptures to their own destruction, he wrote, *"You therefore, beloved, since you know this beforehand, beware lest you also fall from your own steadfastness, being led away with the error of the wicked" (2 Pet. 3:17)*. The word "beware" is defined by Strong's as, "to watch, i.e. be on guard (literally or figuratively); by implication, to preserve, obey, avoid." To "beware" is to be aware of your surroundings. Those who *"know these things"* are responsible for helping others defend themselves. The Christian must *"Be sober, be vigilant; because your adversary the devil walks about like a roaring lion, seeking whom he may devour" (1 Pet. 5:8)*. Unfortunately, the devourer of congregations (Satan) uses his servants who are members of it to undermine its unity. No explorer in the jungle ignores the possibility that the lion could lurk in the shadows. Neither can the congregation forget that her enemy poses an ever-present threat.

Paul ends his second letter to Timothy using the word *"guard,"* which is the same Greek word translated *"beware"* that Peter used. Paul wrote, *"O Timothy! Guard what was committed to your trust, avoiding the profane and idle babblings and contradictions of what is falsely called knowledge — by professing it some have strayed concerning the faith"* (1 Tim. 6:20-21). Paul had entrusted the word of God to Timothy and instructs him to "guard" it against any threat that would cause him or others to stray from the faith. When division results, there has been a failure to beware and guard the unifying principles of God's word.

The leadership of the congregation has a tremendous responsibility in the watch, care, and guarding of the congregation against division. Whether the division is internal, or when Christians behave in a way that separates them from God. God told Ezekiel He had made him a watchman over the house of Israel. And, if he did not warn the people of the evils they were committing, he would suffer severe consequences. *"When I say to the wicked, 'You shall surely die,' and you give him no warning, nor speak to warn the wicked from his wicked way, to save his life, that same wicked man shall die in his iniquity; but his blood I will require at your hand"* (Ezek. 3:18).

> **The leadership of the congregation has a tremendous responsibility in the watch, care, and guarding of the congregation against division.**

God did not authorize men to be elders in His Son's church simply to give them a title or to ensure the financial and business affairs of the congregation were carried out. Their primary responsibility is to guard the flock against any intrusion of something divisive. This includes anyone who promotes anything with the slightest potential to disrupt unity. Paul's writing to Titus defines the qualifications required to serve as an elder. Following these credentials, he states a key purpose for them when he wrote, *"holding fast the faithful word as he has been taught, that he may be able, by sound doctrine, both to exhort and convict those who contradict. For there are many insubordinates, both idle talkers and deceivers, especially those of the circumcision, whose mouths must be stopped, who subvert whole households, teaching things which they ought not, for the sake of dishonest gain" (Titus 1:9-12).* Men without the knowledge of truth and the tenacity to take a stand against the insurgence of divisive brethren are not qualified to lead God's people.

2. Uncompromising Teaching.

Those who shepherd the flock must make teaching about the preservation of unity and the warning signs of division a part of the sheep's diet. The devil uses teaching to promote error and division. The only way to combat his efforts is by teaching the word of God. Paul warned the Ephesian elders, *"For I know this, that after my departure savage wolves will come in among you, not sparing the flock. Also, from among yourselves men will rise up, speaking perverse things, to draw away the disciples after themselves. Therefore watch, and remember that for three years I did not cease to warn everyone night and day with tears" (Acts 20:29-31).* Whether division or its seeds are present, teaching and warning the church about its potential must never cease.

Paul's instruction emphasized to Timothy his duty as a preacher and why he must carry out this role. *"Preach the word! Be ready in season and out of season. Convince, rebuke, exhort, with all longsuffering and teaching. For the time will come when they will not endure sound doctrine, but according to their own desires, because they have itching ears, they will heap up for themselves teachers; and they will turn their ears away from the truth, and be turned aside to fables" (2 Tim. 4:2-4).* There will always be those who will step up and scratch itching ears with preaching what people want to hear. For this reason, the preacher must inform the congregation with truth so that they can identify the slightest threat to unity. John wrote, *"Beloved, do not believe every spirit, but test the spirits, whether they are of God; because many false prophets have gone out into the world" (1 John 4:1).* God's people must have preaching and teaching that equips them with courage and knowledge to test those things influencing them. A lack of firm, decisive, and unequivocal preaching and teaching about moral and religious issues will leave a void that error and division will fill.

Many teach, and some Christians believe it does not matter what you believe. If so, why did Paul and John issue the warnings we just examined? Peter obviously did not subscribe to this thinking either. He wrote, *"But there were also false prophets among the people, even as there will* be false teachers among you, who will secretly bring in destructive heresies, even denying the Lord who bought them, and bring on themselves swift destruction. And many will follow their destructive ways" (2 Pet. 2:1-2). Is it acceptable to believe, "destructive heresies,...deny Jesus?" Obviously not! Especially knowing it results in "swift destruction." Congregations need and deserve teaching and preaching that draws conclusions consistent with the word of God.

3. Discipline.

There are two kinds of discipline—instructive and corrective. Teaching is the instructive discipline a congregation needs to minimize the use of corrective discipline. Unfortunately, leaders and congregations that tolerate substandard preaching and teaching are likely to fail to implement corrective discipline as well.

Faithful Christians need to discontinue close associations with whispering, backbiting, and divisive Christians, lest they be seduced.

Christians need to understand Paul's writing to the Roman Christians regarding actions and attitudes towards those causing division. "Now I urge you, brethren, note those who cause divisions and offenses, contrary to the doctrine which you learned, and avoid them" (Rom. 16:17). The word "note" means "to take aim at" (Strongs). The KJV uses the word "mark." The person who "causes division and offenses contrary to the doctrine of Christ," and refuses to repent, must be exposed to the congregation. If false doctrine is being used, it must be countered with truth. Leaders and congregations must deal with anyone who disrupts or poses a threat to the unity of the congregation. This disruption includes intrusions into matters of judgment or expediency.

In some cases, congregations have friction and division when leadership refuses to address the openly sinful behavior among the members, including those who incite division. Though there were many issues in the church at Corinth causing division, including matters of judgment, they did not seem concerned about an individual committing fornication. In fact, they were "puffed up rather than mourning" (1 Cor. 5:1-11). Paul did not hesitate to expose it and command what the church must do. "But *now I have written to you not to keep company with anyone named a brother, who is sexually immoral, or covetous, or an idolater, or a reviler, or a drunkard, or an extortioner — not even to eat with such a person"* (1 Cor. 5:11). There is not a command in the NT disobeyed any more than this. God demands that intimate social interaction, such as eating with a fellow Christian who is openly practicing sin, must be stopped. This would include anyone who causes or promotes division for any reason.

Why does God require marking and withdrawing from erring or divisive members of His Son's church? Paul answers this question. *"And if any man obeys not our word by this epistle, note that man, and have no company with him, that he may be ashamed. Yet count him not as an enemy, but admonish him as a brother"* (2 Thes. 3:14-15). The stated reason is, *"that he may be ashamed."* God desires that this person repent, and hopefully, the shame of being identified or "marked" will achieve this desired result. A second reason (though not stated in this text) is for the congregation to remove the influence of the erring Christian on other members. Faithful Christians need to discontinue close associations with whispering, backbiting, and divisive Christians, lest they be seduced. And yet there is a third reason. When valuable social ties are severed, hopefully, the erring Christian will equate this with the close tie he is severing with his Heavenly Father. However, when divisive and erring Christians are permitted to mix and mingle with the faithful, sooner or later their evil influence will lead others astray. It is also worth noting that Paul stated, *"Yet count him not as an enemy, but admonish him as a brother."* Congregations must maintain open lines of communication so they can warn the erring Christian and encourage them to repent, thereby restoring their fellowship with God and other Christians. God is willing that all men repent; we must share His desire.

Conclusion

Perhaps we could explore other ways the Bible helps preserve and protect unity. However, being alert, uncompromising in teaching, and using corrective discipline are critical to the peace of a congregation. The design and building of the church are without flaw. It is the introduction of man's thinking, wants, and desires that corrupt and divide it. When man accepts no standard but what the NT teaches, and conforms to it, unity will prevail and division can be restored.

Questions and Discussion

1. What do the words "beware" and "guard" mean, and how do they contribute to congregational unity?

2. How does 1 Pet. 5:8 speak to the preservation of unity?

3. What did God tell Ezekiel he was responsible for, and how are leaders in the church responsible in the same way?

4. Following the qualifications for elders revealed in Titus 1, what responsibilities are commanded, and why?

5. What proactive measure is needed to help prevent division in the congregation?

6. Regarding the matter of division, what must the nature of the preaching and teaching given to the congregation equip its members?

7. What are the two types of discipline the Bible mentions? How does each one help preserve unity?

8. What does the word "note" mean, and how is this command executed?

9. For what reasons should members of the church be "noted" and "withdrawn from"?

10. What is the responsibility of faithful Christians toward those who have been disciplined?

Lesson Eleven

The Eternal Consequences of Division

The detestable effects of division in the church are ugly, heartbreaking, and sinful. However, this should give us pause so we think about the eternal misery and heartache awaiting the perpetrators of division. Neither will those who endorsed or supported their efforts be exempt. As with most sins, the sinner is living in the moment with total disregard for the long-term consequences of their actions.

One cannot find any stronger indictments in the word of God than those leveled at divisive persons. These strong indictments exist because of the ultimate result of division, which means that someone will be separated from God and all that is enduringly good for eternity. Who wants to provoke God to hate them? No one, of course. But divisive persons do just this. Included among the seven things God hates is, *"And one who sows discord among brethren" (Prov. 6:19)*. The person who angers God to the point He hates them must resolve this problem before they leave this life to meet His appointed Judge.

Paul's list of the works of the flesh includes *"hatred, contentions, jealousies...selfish ambitions, dissensions...envy...and the like; of which I tell you beforehand, just as I also told you in time past, that those who practice such things will not inherit the kingdom of God" (Gal. 5:19-21)*. Not that it takes more than one of these sinful traits to be disinherited from the kingdom of God, but nearly every one mentioned in the excerpt quoted from these verses is present when there is division in the church. To be disinherited is to be removed from the will. The Last Will and Testament of Jesus Christ bequeaths salvation to those who obey Him. Those who cause and support division in His church are stripped of their inheritance until they repent.

Those who cause division in the congregation are lawless, in other words, operating outside the law. Jesus used an unmistakable term to describe their eternal destiny. Jesus said, *"Many will say to Me in that day, 'Lord, Lord, have we not prophesied in Your name, cast out demons in Your name, and done many wonders in Your name?' And then I will declare to them, I never knew you; depart from Me, you who practice lawlessness!" (Matt. 7:22-23)*. Those who demonstrated divisive behavior that separated Christians in Jesus' church will be separated from

Him for eternity. Although they may have done some good works, their lawless and divisive actions will tip the scales of Divine Justice in favor of torment. The Hebrew writer reveals the consequences for failing to seek peace when he wrote, *"Pursue peace with all people, and holiness, without which no one will see the Lord"* (Heb. 12:14).

Do those who cause division that separates them from their brethren, and refuse to repent and unify over matters of judgment and expediencies, want to spend eternity with them? Whether they do or not, they will not. When John describes the eternal place of the saved, he writes, *"But there shall by no means enter it anything that defiles, or causes an abomination or a lie, but only those who are written in the Lamb's Book of Life"* (Rev. 21:27). Division defiles and is an abomination to God. This division will end when eternity begins, and the divisive people will not have their names in the Lamb's Book of Life. Those who caused division need not worry about spending eternity with those they did not love enough to unify; they will not be in the same place.

> **Who wants to provoke God to hate them? No one, of course. But divisive persons do just this. Included among the seven things God hates is, *"And one who sows discord among brethren"* (Prov. 6:19).**

Although God will consign divisive people to a place of torment with the devil and his angels, it can be avoided with repentance. Those to whom Paul preached in Athens were reminded that there is hope for the living who engage in idolatrous actions. He said, *"Truly, these times of ignorance God overlooked, but now commands all men everywhere to repent, because He has appointed a day on which He will judge the world in righteousness by the Man whom He has ordained. He has given assurance of this to all by raising Him from the dead"* (Acts 17:30-31). If those who caused or supported division repent, God will forgive them as He does an idolator. If they refuse to repent, they will suffer the consequences when they appear before the Great Judge.

God's mercy is inexhaustible, but it is not offered unless those who desire and need it humble themselves. *"The Lord is near to those who have a broken heart, and saves such as have a contrite spirit" (Psa. 34:17).* King David repented of his sin with Bathsheba, and having her husband killed. His sins gave the enemies of God occasion to blaspheme (2 Sam. 12:14). In David's psalm extolling God's mercy, he wrote, *"The sacrifices of God are a broken spirit, A broken and a contrite heart—These, O God, You will not despise" (Psa. 51:17).*

Conclusion

When one learns they have in any way participated in or endorsed a rupture of the unity of God's people, they have no choice but to repent if they want to go to heaven. And when they do, all those concerned should thank and praise God, and strengthen the penitent.

Questions and Discussion

1. In what way(s) might the earthly effects of division be compared to the eternal consequences?

2. Review the works of the flesh in Gal. 5:19-21. Discuss how each one might contribute to division and its consequences.

3. Define the word "lawless" that Jesus used, and how does this apply to a divisive person? And what does Jesus declare is the result?

4. What does the Hebrew writer say the consequences are for not living in peace with all men? Compare with Matt. 5:9.

5. Read Rev. 21:27. How can this be applied to those who cause division?

6. What does God require of those who want to go to heaven, but have caused or participated in division?

7. Read 1 Sam. 13:14; Acts 13:22; and Psa. 51. Given all of King David's sins, how did he endear himself to God? What is the application today?

Lesson Twelve

The Reward of Unity

In this series, we have studied the example of unity, the causes and effects of division, and the eternal consequences for those who cause division. It is only fitting to conclude this study of *The Anatomy of Unity and Division* by examining the reward awaiting those who are unified with one another and with God, according to truth. As difficult as the struggle can be to maintain unity, the efforts of those who have striven to preserve it will not go unnoticed by God. The battle for unity should be fought in view of the fact that God "is a rewarder of those who diligently seek Him" (Heb. 11:6). Therefore, let us examine the reward of unity.

To preface this study, we need to be reminded that "unity" by God's definition is not simply "agreeing to disagree." "Unity" is the result of everyone believing and obeying the one standard set forth by God in the NT. Paul defines the nature of unity when he wrote, *"Now I plead with you, brethren, by the name of our Lord Jesus Christ, that you all speak the same thing, and that there be no divisions among you, but that you be perfectly joined together in the same mind and in the same judgment"* (1 Cor. 1:10). *"By the name of the Lord Jesus Christ"* means by His authority. Therefore, Paul's insistence that the Corinthians have no division, speak the same thing, have the same mind and same judgment came from Jesus, not some optional idea contrived by Paul.

Heaven is the destiny for those who pursue peace. We know that no division will be there. In this life, there is always the potential for division or unrest in every relationship, but not in heaven. It is difficult to comprehend an existence in an unending realm of peace and unity. We will not be concerned with having a watchful eye for the foe. God will banish our foe and his servants from the presence of the peacemakers for eternity. *"There remains therefore a rest for the people of God. For he who has entered His rest has himself also ceased from his works as God did from His"* (Heb. 4:9-10). God will reward the labors and heartaches of the faithful who struggled for peace and unity with rest. The *"people of God"* are those God calls His children. God's spiritual family is made up of those who made every effort to maintain a peaceful relationship with Him and His family. Jesus said, *"Blessed are the peacemakers, for they shall be called sons of God"* (Matt. 5:9). The realm of eternity for the faithful is described in terms that should compel everyone to become a member of the family of God and remain faithful. John describes this realm by informing us of what "is not" there. *"And I heard a loud voice from heaven saying, Behold, the tabernacle of God is with men, and He will dwell with them, and they shall be His people. God Himself will be with them and be their God. And God will wipe away every tear from their eyes; there shall be no more death, nor sorrow, nor crying. There shall be no more pain, for the former things have passed away" (Rev. 21:3-4).*

What is heaven worth? Anything we must endure in this life. The Christians living in the first century not only endured the effects of divisive brethren and false teachers, but also immeasurable persecution from civil governments and other religious groups. For these reasons, Paul told the Roman Christians, *"For I consider that the sufferings of this present time are not worthy to be compared with the glory which shall be revealed in us" (Rom. 8:18).*

To be at peace with God and have the right to anticipate living in eternity with Him depends on our efforts to be at peace with one another.

Heaven is the ultimate reward for those who have made and preserved peace, because it is there that God and Christ dwell. However, the word of God has also promised that God will be with those in this life who live in peace with Him and others. *"Finally, brethren, farewell. Become complete. Be of good comfort, be of one mind, live in peace; and the God of love and peace will be with you" (2 Cor. 13:11).*

Though Paul's list of Christian virtues in Philippians 4 does not specifically mention peace and unity, the clause, *"if there is anything praiseworthy,"* would include both. And the others identified in this text certainly describe the qualities of a person who pursues peace and does not promote division. The climax of this list is the statement describing the result of the faithful peacekeeper, *"the God of peace will be with you."* Note the text: *"Finally, brethren, whatever things are true, whatever things are noble, whatever things are just, whatever things are pure, whatever things are lovely, whatever things are of good report, if there is any virtue and if there is anything praiseworthy—meditate on these things. The things which you learned and received and heard and saw in me, these do, and the God of peace will be with you" (Phil. 4:8-9).* No other comfort in this life compares with knowing that God is with you. When Jesus comforted His disciples who were troubled, He said, *"If anyone loves Me, he will keep My word; and My Father will love him, and We will come to him and make Our home with him" (John 14:23).*

Conclusion

To be at peace with God and have the right to anticipate living in eternity with Him depends on our efforts to be at peace with one another. We only have absolute control over one-half of any relationship. However, how we treat, communicate, and respect others directly affects how the other party may react. We can either bring out the best or the worst in others. Our goal should be to strive as peacemakers in all our interactions with others, and this is especially true in our relationships with fellow Christians. The church is the only organization for which the Son of God died. We should never want to be found doing anything that ruptures it. Paul wrote, "If it is possible, as much as depends on you, live peaceably with all men" (Rom. 12:18).

Questions and Discussion

1. Who does God reward, and how does this apply to the subject of this lesson?

2. Why is "agreeing to disagree" in spiritual matters unacceptable?

3. Read and discuss each aspect of 1 Cor. 1:10.

4. How does the Hebrew writer describe what awaits those who have labored for God?

5. In what ways can we implement Matt. 5:9?

6. From Rev. 21:3-4, what things are mentioned that "are not" in heaven, and how can each apply to division or unity among God's people?

7. What is the result (in this life) of living in peace and unity? (2 Cor. 13:11 and John 14:23)

8. In our relationship with our brethren and others, discuss how our actions and attitudes affect the ability for unity and peace to exist.

9. To what extent should a Christian pursue peace with his brethren or others if he wants to go to heaven (Rom. 12:18)?

10. What does Paul say about the comparison between the sufferings of this life when contrasted with Heaven?

Lesson Thirteen

Review Questions

1. How do the Father, the Son, and the Holy Spirit provide an example for men to be unified?

2. Though having different roles, describe what each member of the Godhead does for the salvation of man.

3. How can we be sure the unity of God's people is not optional?

4. How was the cost paid so that all men can be unified with God and one another?

5. What is the debt all men owe that they can never satisfy?

6. What specific statements did Jesus use when He prayed for our unity?

7. Why is "agreeing to disagree" not God's perspective of unity for His people?

8. List and review verses teaching what the only basis for unity with God and others must be.

9. Why is it impossible for man to create a plan or system that unifies him with God or man?

10. What motives are usually present when division occurs in the church?

11. What are some methods used to promote division in the church?

12. List some verses that warn of the eternal consequences of division.

13. What are some of the consequences Christians and congregations endure because of division?

14. What is the responsibility of members of the church when confronted with divisive communication?

15. What proactive measures should elders implement concerning unity and division?

16. What action should elders take toward members causing and promoting division in the church?

17. What attitude(s) should each member of the church have that preserves unity?

18. What do you believe are three major causes for brethren dividing over matters of judgment or expediency?

19. What is the only reason God will justify His faithful servants when they separate from one another?

20. What key virtue is absent when division occurs in the church?

21. Can unity among divided brethren be restored? If so, how?